EXPLORING COUNTRIES

EXPLORANDO PAÍSES

COSTA RICA

Tracy Vonder Brink

Translated by/Traducción de Santiago Ochoa

TABLE OF CONTENTS

ÍNDICE

A Crabtree Seedlings Book
Un libro de El Semillero de Crabtree

Crabtree Publishing
crabtreebooks.com

School-to-Home Support for Caregivers and Teachers

This book helps children grow by letting them practice reading. Here are a few guiding questions to help the reader with building his or her comprehension skills. Possible answers appear here in red.

Before Reading:

- What do I think this book is about?
- *I think this book is about Costa Rica.*
- *I think this book is about the beaches of Costa Rica.*

- What do I want to learn about this topic?
- *I want to learn about the animals that live in Costa Rica.*
- *I want to learn about the activities people do in Costa Rica.*

During Reading:

- I wonder why...
- *I wonder why there are volcanoes in Costa Rica.*
- *I wonder why there are so many forests in Costa Rica.*

- What have I learned so far?
- *I have learned that San José is the capital of Costa Rica.*
- *I have learned that jaguars are the biggest wild cats in Costa Rica.*

After Reading:

- What details did I learn about this topic?
- *I have learned that Costa Rica is in Central America.*
- *I have learned that San José is more than 200 years old.*

- Read the book again and look for the vocabulary words.
- *I see the word **capital** on page 4, and the word **erupted** on page 18. The other glossary words are on pages 22 and 23.*

Apoyo escolar para cuidadores y profesores

Este libro ayuda a los niños a crecer al permitirles practicar la lectura. A continuación se presentan algunas preguntas orientativas para ayudar al lector a desarrollar su capacidad de comprensión. Las posibles respuestas que aparecen aquí están en color rojo.

Antes de leer:

- ¿De qué creo que trata este libro?
- *Creo que este libro trata sobre Costa Rica.*
- *Creo que este libro trata sobre las playas de Costa Rica.*

- ¿Qué quiero aprender sobre este tema?
- *Quiero aprender sobre los animales que viven en Costa Rica.*
- *Quiero aprender sobre las actividades de la gente en Costa Rica.*

Durante la lectura:

- Me pregunto por qué...
- *Me pregunto por qué hay volcanes en Costa Rica.*
- *Me pregunto por qué hay tantas selvas en Costa Rica.*

- ¿Qué he aprendido hasta ahora?
- *He aprendido que San José es la capital de Costa Rica.*
- *He aprendido que los jaguares son los felinos salvajes más grandes de Costa Rica.*

Después de leer:

- ¿Qué detalles he aprendido sobre este tema?
- *He aprendido que Costa Rica está en Centroamérica.*
- *He aprendido que San José tiene más de 200 años.*

- Vuelve a leer el libro y busca las palabras del glosario.
- *Veo la palabra **capital** en la página 4 y las palabras **hizo erupción** en la página 18. Las otras palabras del glosario se encuentran en las páginas 22 y 23.*

Costa Rica is a small country.
It is in **Central America**.

Costa Rica es un país pequeño.
Queda en **Centroamérica**.

San José is the **capital**
of Costa Rica.
The city is more than
200 years old.

San José es la **capital**
de Costa Rica.
La ciudad tiene más
de 200 años.

Most people in Costa Rica speak Spanish.

En Costa Rica la mayoría de la gente habla español.

San José has a large market. Shoppers buy food, clothes, and other goods there.

San José tiene un gran mercado. Allí, las personas compran alimentos, ropa y otros productos.

Costa Rica has many forests.

Costa Rica tiene muchas selvas.

They cover more than half of the country's land.

Las selvas cubren más de la mitad del territorio del país.

These forests are important to Earth. They take in a gas called **carbon dioxide**.

Estas selvas son importantes para la Tierra. Absorben un gas llamado **dióxido de carbono**.

Factories and cars put out carbon dioxide as they burn fuel.

Las fábricas y los autos emiten dióxido de carbono a medida que queman combustible.

They put out oxygen that people and animals breathe.

Las selvas devuelven el oxígeno que respiran las personas y los animales.

Rain forests are home to many animals.

Las **selvas tropicales** son el hogar de muchos animales.

Scarlet macaws fly from tree to tree.

Las guacamayas rojas vuelan de árbol en árbol.

Jaguars hunt in the dark. They are the biggest wild cats in Costa Rica.

Los jaguares cazan en la oscuridad. Son los felinos salvajes más grandes de Costa Rica.

Jaguars hunt on land and in water. They eat deer, fish, and many other animals.

Los jaguares cazan en la tierra y en el agua. Se alimentan de ciervos, peces y muchos otros animales.

Costa Rica has beautiful waterfalls. One is called La Paz. Its name means peace.

Costa Rica tiene cascadas muy bonitas. Una de ellas se llama La Paz.

Costa Rica has more than 60 volcanoes. The Arenal volcano **erupted** many times. Now it is quiet.

Costa Rica tiene más de 60 volcanes. El volcán Arenal **hizo erupción** muchas veces. Ahora está inactivo.

Beaches line the **coast**. The sand is white and soft. Costa Rica has so much to see!

Las playas bordean la **costa**. Su arena es blanca y suave. ¡En Costa Rica hay mucho que ver!

Glossary / Glosario

capital (KAP-i-tl): The city where the government of a country or a state is located

capital: La ciudad donde se encuentra el gobierno de un país o Estado.

carbon dioxide (KAAR-buhn dai-OX-side): A gas made when people and animals breathe out or when some fuels are burned

dióxido de carbono: Un gas que se produce cuando las personas y los animales exhalan o cuando se queman algunos combustibles.

Central America (SEN-truhl uh-MEH-ruh-kuh): The region between Mexico and South America

Centroamérica: La región situada entre México y Sudamérica.

coast (kohst): The land next to the ocean or sea

costa: La franja de tierra situada junto al océano o al mar.

erupted (ee-RUPT-ed): Suddenly sent out lava, ash, rocks, or other material

hizo erupción: De repente expulsó lava, cenizas, rocas u otros materiales.

rain forests (RAYN-faw-ruhsts): Dense, tropical forests that have large amounts of rainfall

selvas tropicales: Bosques densos en los que llueve en grandes cantidades.

Index

Índice analítico

About the Author

Tracy Vonder Brink loves to visit new places. She has never been to Costa Rica, but she has read a lot about rain forests. She lives in Cincinnati with her husband, two daughters, and two rescue dogs.

Acerca de la autora

A Tracy Vonder Brink le encanta visitar lugares nuevos. Nunca ha estado en Costa Rica, pero ha leído mucho sobre las selvas tropicales. Vive en Cincinnati con su esposo, sus dos hijas y dos perros de rescate.

Crabtree Publishing

crabtreebooks.com 800-387-7650

Hardcover 978-1-0398-6928-8
Paperback 978-1-0398-6907-3
Ebook (pdf) 978-1-0398-6949-3
Epub 978-1-0398-6970-7

Printed in the U.S.A./CP2025

Published in Canada
Publicado en Canadá
Crabtree Publishing
616 Welland Avenue
St. Catharines, Ontario
L2M 5V6

Published in the United States
Publicado en los Estados Unidos
Crabtree Publishing
347 Fifth Avenue
Suite 1402-145
New York, NY 10016

Written by/Escrito por: Tracy Vonder Brink
Designer/Diseñador: Under the Oaks Media
Proofreader/Correctora de pruebas: Melissa Boyce
Translated by/Traducción de: Santiago Ochoa
Spanish-language copyediting and proofreading/
Maquetación y corrección en español: Base Tres
Coordinador de producción/Production manager:
Candice Cambell

Photographs/Fotografías: Shutterstock: DeLoyd Huenink: cover; Vlad Ispas: p. 3; mbrand85: p. 5; Inspired by maps: p. 7; Simon Dannhauer: p. 9; Cocos. Bounty: p. 10-11; Artem Oleshko: p. 10; gary yim: p. 12; G-Arbul: p. 13; Jamen Percy: p. 15; Dmitry Burlakov: p. 17; Bos11: p. 18-19; Tami Feed: p. 21

Library and Archives Canada Cataloguing in Publication Available at the Library and Archives Canada

Library of Congress Cataloging-in-Publication Data
Available at the Library of Congress